Gorilla
Watching Tours

T0066379

Rob Waring, *Series Editor*

HEINLE
CENGAGE Learning

Australia • Brazil • Japan • Korea • Mexico • Singapore • Spain • United Kingdom • United States

Words to Know

This story is set in Africa. It happens in Uganda, [yugændə] in the Bwindi Impenetrable [bwɪndi ɪmpɛnɪtrəbəl] National Park.

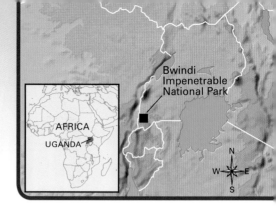

Bwindi Impenetrable National Park

AFRICA
UGANDA

A **An Unusual Type of Tour.** Read the paragraph. Then match each word with the correct definition.

The Bwindi Impenetrable National Park is well-known for being the home of the mountain gorilla. Ecologists often go there to study the gorillas. However, recently many tourists have also come to the area. They pay guides to go with them into the forest. They want to watch gorillas in their natural environment. The money from these gorilla watching tours helps to keep the gorillas safe. It helps to pay for the conservation of these interesting animals.

1. national park _____	**a.** the protection of plants, animals, or natural areas
2. gorilla _____	**b.** a large area with many trees
	c. a visitor who travels for fun
3. ecologist _____	**d.** a person whose job is showing places to visitors
4. tourist _____	**e.** a special area where nature is protected
5. guide _____	**f.** a large animal that lives in western Africa
6. forest _____	**g.** a person who studies the relationship between living things and their environments
7. conservation _____	

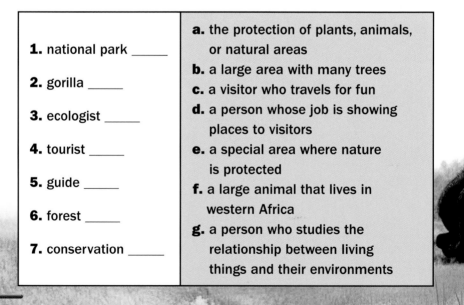

B **Gorilla Facts.** Read the facts about gorillas. Then write the correct underlined word or phrase next to each definition.

A gorilla is a kind of ape. Gorillas live in groups, or families, like human beings. The leader of each group or family of gorillas is a large male gorilla, called a silverback. Gorillas make their homes by building something called a nest. While the number of mountain gorillas in the world is staying the same now, their numbers were declining in past years. There are very few left in the world.

1. a home made from parts of trees or plants: _____
2. the biggest or strongest male gorilla: _____
3. going down; getting lower: _____
4. people: _____
5. an animal which is like a large monkey with no tail: _____

guide

tourists

forest

mountain gorillas

The name 'Bwindi' means 'place of darkness.' The forests of the Bwindi Impenetrable National Park, Uganda, are certainly big and dark. This is especially true for a group of tourists very early in the morning. They're getting ready to start a long day of gorilla watching. The group hopes to have a chance to see gorillas in their natural forest environment.

As the tourists start their slow walk into the thick forest, they learn quickly that this is not going to be easy. Medad is their guide; his job is to show them where the gorillas are. As they walk, he explains where they're going to find the gorillas. He says: "These animals are called mountain gorillas, and mostly you find them on tops of mountains. So on our way, we should expect to be going up and down, up and down..." The group soon finds out that this is certainly true!

CD 1, Track 03

The tourists continue walking. They realize that they will probably have to walk a long way to see the gorillas. Then, suddenly, Medad gets a report. It's about the thirteen members of the group of gorillas called the 'M' group! They were seen at the far side of the forest. That means that they are many kilometers away.

"Here we go," says one of the tourists, and the group starts walking towards the 'M' group. They continue walking for a few hours. Finally, they reach a big hill that is covered in **mud**.[1] It's a very difficult walk, but the group makes it up the hill. They continue walking and looking, but they still don't see any gorillas.

---

[1]**mud:** a soft combination of water and earth

Behavioral ecologist Michele Goldsmith has come along on the tour. Goldsmith's job is studying how gorillas act in their natural environment. She's been studying Bwindi's gorillas for five years.

Goldsmith knows where to find gorillas. She says that where they stay often depends on their food: "If they're in a place with very **dense vegetation**[2] that they're eating, they won't go very far. Sometimes they'll travel 300 [to] 400 **meters**[3] in a day. And then if there's maybe a preferred site they want to visit, they'll travel more than a kilometer."

---

[2]**dense vegetation:** a lot of plants
[3]**meter:** 1 meter = 3.3 feet; 1000 meters = 1 kilometer

The group keeps looking for the gorillas. There are more than 300 gorillas living in Bwindi Impenetrable National Park, but it's possible that the group won't see any of them. After some time, however, the tourists find gorilla nests, and gorilla **droppings**.[4] These are encouraging signs—the gorillas can't be far away!

The group continues walking, but stops very quickly. They've suddenly realized something. They are not 'watching' anything—something's watching them!

---

[4]**droppings:** waste produced by animals and birds

Predict

Answer the questions. Then scan page 12 to check your answers.

1. Who is watching the tourists?

2. What will the tourists do?

A young gorilla slowly stands up to look at the tourists. The tourists then realize that there are several gorillas in the area. They have found the group!

It starts raining, and the gorillas walk away to find **shelter**[5] from the rain under some big trees. The tourists follow carefully and try to get close to the gorilla family. The silverback—the big male gorilla—rests alone. Nearby, the tourists can see a mother with two young gorillas. The group is entertained by the young gorillas as they play in the trees. The tourists sit down for a while to watch them. This is exactly what they were hoping to see!

---

[5]**shelter:** protection from the weather

The gorillas go under the trees to find shelter from the rain.

When the rain stops, the gorillas start to move again. First the silverback leaves. Then, a mother goes with her baby on her back. Several small gorillas follow the larger and older gorillas. The younger ones have lots of energy! They run and play around the other gorillas as they move through the forest.

Since 1993 small groups of people have visited these apes almost every day. It's easy to see that these gorillas are used to human beings; they're relaxed when people are around them. This sense of comfort with people allows the tourists time to watch the gorillas. They can closely observe these beautiful animals in their own environment. But what do the gorillas do all day?

The gorillas spend most of their time eating. They eat leaves, **bark**,[6] fruit, and other plants. While the older gorillas eat, the younger gorillas play in the trees.

Finally, the silverback goes into the forest again. It's time for the tourists to leave. It's also time to end a very interesting day. This group of tourists was very fortunate. They were actually able to see gorillas in nature.

---

[6]**bark:** the hard outer covering of a tree

Scan for Information

Scan pages 14 and 16 to find the information.

1. In which year did people first come to visit the Bwindi gorillas?

2. What do gorillas spend most of their time doing?

3. What are four things gorillas eat?

The mountain gorillas of the Bwindi Impenetrable National Park are beautiful animals. Unfortunately, there are only about 700 mountain gorillas left in the world. The money from gorilla watching tours like this one may help conservation efforts. Will it be enough? No one knows.

In fact, there are many questions about the future of the mountain gorilla. Will the world find better methods of protecting them? Will their numbers increase or decline? Will the money from gorilla watching tours really help save them? Or will the beautiful gorillas of Bwindi **disappear**[7] from these forests forever?

---

[7]**disappear:** go away; leave suddenly

After You Read

1. What are the tourists thinking when they start their tour?
   A. The park feels big and dark.
   B. The gorillas are dangerous.
   C. It's late and cold.
   D. The gorillas are near.

2. In paragraph 1 on page 4, the word 'chance' means:
   A. look
   B. experience
   C. opportunity
   D. time

3. In paragraph 1 on page 7, the word 'they were seen' refers to the:
   A. tourists
   B. trees
   C. guides
   D. gorillas

4. According to Michele Goldsmith, which is true about the gorillas?
   A. They will not travel for food.
   B. They stay near food.
   C. They don't like the dense vegetation in the forest.
   D. They will travel more than a kilometer to find food.

5. Which is NOT a good heading for page 10?
   A. Good Signs, Getting Closer
   B. Apes See Tourists First
   C. Large Park, Long Walk
   D. No Gorillas to Watch Yet

6. The tourists finally found _____ gorillas.
   A. some
   B. any
   C. no
   D. most

7. Which kind of gorilla do the tourists NOT see?

    A. a mother

    B. a young gorilla

    C. a grandfather

    D. a silverback

8. In paragraph 2 on page 12, what does the word 'carefully' mean?

    A. quickly

    B. quietly

    C. closely

    D. suddenly

9. The gorillas probably feel that human beings are:

    A. happy

    B. dangerous

    C. unusual

    D. safe

10. It is important that gorillas have a sense of comfort with people because:

    A. The gorillas must eat often.

    B. Gorillas are beautiful.

    C. People come to see them often.

    D. People are not very careful.

11. Why were the tourists fortunate to visit the gorillas?

    A. because gorillas don't like people

    B. because there are so few gorillas

    C. because the gorillas don't like rain

    D. because the park isn't big enough

12. What is the main purpose of this story?

    A. to show a beautiful animal that needs help

    B. to discuss tourism in Uganda

    C. to teach about the silverback

    D. to introduce a Ugandan national park

The History of the National Park System

Today, there are thousands of national parks all over the world. The world's first national park was started in 1864. In that year, the United States government gave a large piece of land to the state of California. They asked the state to create a special park to protect the mountains and forests in the area. The trees in this area are called sequoias. The biggest ones are over one hundred meters high. They are the tallest living things in the world and are not found anywhere else on Earth.

Some sequoia trees are over one hundred meters high.

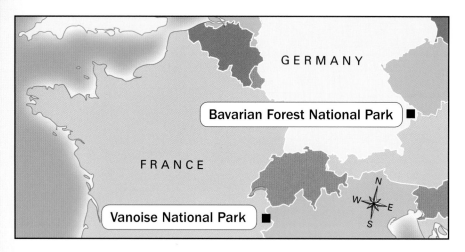

Conservationists in other countries saw what happened in California and soon began to do the same. Today Europe has over 350 national parks. The first one in France, Vanoise National Park, was created in 1963 because the government wanted to stop a plan to build a large tourist project there. The idea of creating a national park was first discussed in the 1940s, but people couldn't agree on what size to make the park. They also had different ideas on whether to put human or animal needs first. Ecologists worked with the government to finally agree on a plan that protected the animals, while still allowing some tourism.

The first national park in Germany opened in 1970. Like the first California park, the Bavarian Forest National Park was created to protect mountains and trees. It is the largest area of protected forest in Europe. The park has shelters where visitors can spend a night close to nature. In some places high up in the mountains, there are steps cut into the rock. This makes it easier for tourists to get to the top. Thousands of tourists go to the park each year. They walk through the attractive woods and enjoy the wonderful mountain views.

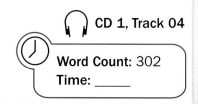

CD 1, Track 04

Word Count: 302
Time: _____

Vocabulary List

ape (3, 14)

bark (16)

conservation (2, 18)

decline (3, 18)

dense vegetation (8)

disappear (18)

droppings (10)

ecologist (2, 8)

forest (2, 4, 7, 14, 16, 18)

gorilla (2, 3, 4, 7, 8, 10, 12, 13, 14, 16, 17, 18)

guide (2, 4)

human being (3, 14)

meter (8)

mud (7)

national park (2, 4, 10, 18)

nest (3, 10)

shelter (12, 13)

silverback (3, 12, 14, 16)

tourist (2, 4, 7, 10, 12, 14, 16)